Barefoot Dancer

Barefoot Dancer

the story of
Isadora Duncan

BARBARA O'CONNOR

Carolrhoda Books, Inc./Minneapolis

For my parents, who paid for all those dancing lessons,
and
For Jill, editor extraordinaire

Carolrhoda Books, Inc. c/o The Lerner Group
241 First Avenue North, Minneapolis, Minnesota 55401

Library of Congress Cataloging-in-Publication Data

O'Connor, Barbara.
   Barefoot dancer : the story of Isadora Duncan / Barbara O'Connor.
      p. cm.
   Includes bibliographical references (p.).
   Summary: Describes the life of the modern dancer who created a
spontaneous, free-form dance style accompanied by literary readings
and non-dance music.
   ISBN 0-87614-807-0
   1. Duncan, Isadora, 1877–1927—Juvenile literature. 2. Dancers—
United States—Biography—Juvenile literature. [1. Duncan, Isadora,
1877–1927. 2. Dancers.] I. Title.
GV1785.D8027   1994
792.8'028'092—dc20
[B]   93-14312
                                                                 CIP
                                                                  AC

Manufactured in the United States of America
        1 2 3 4 5 6 - I/JR - 99 98 97 96 95 94

Contents

Isadora believed she was born a dancer. This photo was taken when she was three years old.

I

A Family of
Artists

During the summer of 1887 in San Francisco, California, visitors to the seaside were sometimes met by a rather unusual sight. A young girl danced at the water's edge, her wet dress clinging to her bare legs and her long hair blowing freely in the breeze.

Those seaside visitors probably thought such behavior was improper and unladylike. But the girl paid no attention. She was too busy mimicking the motions of the wind, the waves, the birds. She swayed gracefully on the wet sand, leaping, twirling, and posing as if she heard music those disapproving observers could not.

That dancing girl was ten-year-old Isadora Duncan. Later in her life, when asked when she first began to dance, she would reply, "In my mother's womb." Though some might find such an answer hard to believe, it is surely true that she began dancing at a very early age.

Isadora was born on May 27, 1877, in a grand house

on the corner of Geary and Taylor Streets in San Francisco. Eagerly awaiting her arrival were her sister, Elizabeth, and her two brothers, Augustin and Raymond. Her father, Joseph Duncan, was a hardworking banker with a talent for making money quickly. Unfortunately, he usually lost it just as quickly. When Isadora was only five months old, Joseph's bank, the Pioneer Land and Loan Bank, went bankrupt. Joseph left home and went into hiding. He didn't want to be around when the police discovered that he had lied about how much money the bank had held. In February 1878, Joseph was caught and charged with fraud and forgery.

Isadora's mother, Dora, was devastated. What a fine mess her husband had left her in—four young children and no money. This was not the kind of life she'd planned for her family, but she would get along without him. Eventually she divorced him.

Without Joseph to help support the family, Dora struggled to make ends meet. She got up at the first hint of daylight to knit caps and mittens to sell. Then she left to give piano lessons in the homes of wealthy families. But still there was never enough money to pay the rent. Isadora's first years were spent moving from one cheap apartment to another. When Dora would tell her children to start packing, they wouldn't ask why. They knew they were being evicted again.

Dora Duncan usually worked until long past dark, but when she got home, she was rarely too tired to sit down at her own piano and play for her children. An accomplished pianist, Dora filled their tiny apartment with the

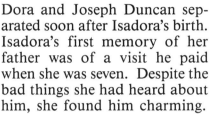

Dora and Joseph Duncan separated soon after Isadora's birth.
Isadora's first memory of her
father was of a visit he paid
when she was seven. Despite the
bad things she had heard about
him, she found him charming.

sonatas of Ludwig van Beethoven and the waltzes of
Franz Schubert. Then she would sing or read or recite
poetry. Dora couldn't give her children fancy clothes or
expensive toys, but she gave them her love of art.

Isadora loved those "enchanted" evenings. Not content to be an idle listener, she twirled and pranced about
the room or acted out a favorite poem. "It was owing
to the heroic and adventurous spirit of my mother that
[my art] was not stifled," Isadora claimed.

Preferring the fun and creative education she received
at home, Isadora hated the confinement of a schoolroom.
She fidgeted and daydreamed and counted the minutes
until three o'clock. "When I could escape from the
prison of school, I was free," she said. "I could wander

alone by the sea and follow my own fantasies."

While many of their friends lived under the strict rule of servants or governesses, the Duncan children spent their afternoons carefree and unsupervised. Far from feeling alone or neglected, Isadora considered herself lucky. "It is certainly to this wild, untrammelled life of my childhood that I owe the inspiration of the dance I created, which was but the expression of freedom. I was never subjected to the continual 'don'ts' which it seems to me make children's lives a misery."

As a young girl, Isadora knew poverty, but she never knew shyness. She loved dancing for the children in her neighborhood. She enjoyed showing the little ones how to wave their arms gracefully in the air or prance about on tiptoe. Happy to have their children occupied and out of trouble, the neighborhood mothers began to pay Isadora a small sum to give dancing lessons in her home.

Isadora loved running her little dancing school. Her sister, Elizabeth, helped teach, and her mother played the piano. Isadora taught her students popular "society dances"—waltzes, mazurkas, and polkas. But what she liked best was making up her own dances. Isadora had a vivid imagination and a flair for the dramatic that the children loved. One of the first dances she taught her class was performed to Henry Wadsworth Longfellow's poem "The Arrow and the Song." While Isadora stood in a corner passionately reciting, "I shot an arrow into the air, / It fell to earth, I know not where," the children danced about the room, shooting invisible arrows from their make-believe bows.

At twelve years old, Isadora was a student, a teacher, and a performer.

Thinking her daughter would benefit from formal dance training, Dora enrolled Isadora in ballet school. But Isadora had no interest in the stiff formality of ballet or the discipline of a formal dance school. She thought ballet was "ugly and against nature."

"I dreamed of a different dance," she said. She preferred to dance alone by the ocean or in the meadows near her home. Fascinated by the motion in nature, she liked to imitate the swaying poppies or the soaring birds. With free-flowing movements, she danced in the wind, waving her arms dramatically over her head.

By the time Isadora was about thirteen years old, her neighborhood business—and her income—had grown considerably. She had always thought school was a waste of time, and she finally convinced her mother that her time was better spent making money for the family. With her mother's consent, Isadora quit school.

The end of her formal education did not mean the end of learning for Isadora. She was blessed with avid curiosity, a passion for the arts, and a family with a healthy respect for new ideas. An enthusiastic reader, Isadora read everything she could find at the library, including books by Dickens, Thackeray, and Shakespeare. Often she sat up all night reading. The next day, after she finished teaching her dance classes, she would hurry to the library for more. "No matter how many miles we were from it," she said, "I ran or danced or skipped there and back."

In 1893, when Isadora was sixteen, her dancing school received an unexpected boost. Her father, Joseph, surprised Dora and their four children by presenting them with a beautiful mansion on the corner of Sutter and Van Ness Streets in San Francisco. He had just made a great deal of money, and perhaps he felt guilty for deserting his family. He was living in Los Angeles, California, and had remarried. He had made and lost a fortune several times since the Pioneer Bank's collapse.

The Duncan children had never known such grandeur. Their new home had a tennis court, a barn, a windmill, and many rooms with big fireplaces. At last Isadora had room to run a real dancing school.

While Isadora was busy setting up her new studio, her brother Augustin built a theater in the big barn behind the house. Each week in their family theater, the children gave performances for the neighborhood. They performed comedy plays together. Augustin recited poetry. And of course, Isadora danced. The family was finally able to devote their time to being true artists. Isadora's mother had once complained, "Why must all four [children] be artists and not one practical?" But in reality, she must have been pleased, for even Isadora knew that it was her mother's own "beautiful and restless spirit" that made them artists.

The Duncans' theater was so successful with their neighbors that before long, the company of four, with Dora as their pianist, took their show on the road to the nearby towns of Santa Clara, Santa Rosa, and Santa Barbara. Isadora had never been happier than she was when performing her own dances for an audience. She began to dream of a career in the theater. But the Duncans' luck was not to hold out. Two years later, Joseph once again lost his fortune, and he was forced to sell their beautiful home.

Early in 1895, the Duncans found themselves back in a cramped rented apartment with no money. Isadora had had enough of this life. Something had to change. San Francisco was just not the place for her, she decided.

If she was ever going to be a professional artist, she would have to leave. Isadora took to the streets, determined to find a job with a traveling theatrical company. At last she managed to arrange an audition.

The morning of the audition, Isadora was nervous and excited. Wearing her favorite costume, a white Greek tunic, she walked out onto a big, bare, black stage. While Dora played Felix Mendelssohn's *Songs without Words,* Isadora gave a passionate and emotional performance. When she finished, the manager was silent for a long time. Isadora's heart pounded as she waited for his decision. Finally, he turned to her mother. "This sort of thing is no good for a theater. It's more for a church. I advise you to take your little girl home."

Isadora was disappointed, but she wasn't about to give up. She went right home and called the Duncan clan together. They must look elsewhere, she told them. They must go east. She and her mother would go first. Once she found a job and began earning money, the others could follow. Isadora was lucky that her family believed in her. They were convinced that their little sister had something new to offer to the world of dance. Someday, they knew, she would be rich and famous.

And so it was agreed. Isadora would go to Chicago to find fame and fortune.

II

A New York Beginning

Eighteen-year-old Isadora arrived in Chicago on a hot June day in 1895 with twenty-five dollars, some of her grandmother's old jewelry, and complete confidence that she would find the perfect job right away. A few weeks later, her money had been spent, the jewelry had been pawned, and her perfect job was nowhere in sight. Day after day, Isadora walked the city streets, carrying her white tunic and auditioning for every theater manager who would see her. Each time, she was told that her dancing was very lovely, "but not for the theater."

As if reliving their hard-luck days in San Francisco, Isadora and her mother found themselves unable to pay the rent. But Isadora was not ready to give up yet. She took the Irish lace collar off her dress and sold it for ten dollars—enough to pay for a month's rent, with a little left over for a box of tomatoes.

A few days later, Isadora read in the newspaper that

Augustin Daly, a well-known theater manager from New York, was in town. Here was her big chance. She would convince him to hire her. Afternoons and evenings, she stood outside the stage door of the theater, waiting to speak to him. When she was finally allowed in, she boldly informed him that his show was not complete without her. "I bring to your theater the vital soul that it lacks," she told him, "the soul of the dancer."

It worked. He told her to report to his theater in New York by the first of October. Isadora ran all the way home, threw open the door, and announced, "At last someone appreciates me, Mamma."

Elizabeth and Augustin joined Isadora and their mother in Chicago, and the four of them boarded the train for New York. They were "wild with excitement and happy expectations." Isadora's career as a famous dancer was about to begin.

As soon as her family was settled in a cheap boarding-house in Manhattan, Isadora reported to the theater. She could hardly wait to get started. By the end of the day, however, she felt disappointed and deceived. Her part in the show was not dancing at all, but pantomime, which Isadora did not consider art. Pantomime merely used gestures to represent words. To Isadora, dancing expressed not just words, but emotions and images.

"I took [the part] home to study," she later recalled, "but the whole thing seemed to me very stupid and quite unworthy of my ambitions and ideals." The part may have been stupid, but it would pay the rent. Reluctantly, Isadora performed her role.

Two months later, the show ended, and the theater troupe began to prepare for its next project, Shakespeare's *A Midsummer Night's Dream.* To Isadora's dismay, the part she was offered was that of a fairy. "My ideas on the dance were to express the feelings and emotions of humanity," she wrote in her memoirs. "I was not at all interested in fairies." But at least this was a dancing part. She would take it.

Isadora in costume for *A Midsummer Night's Dream,* 1895

Dressed in a long, loose dress of white and gold gauze, with two tinsel wings flapping on her back, Isadora danced around the stage. The audience loved her and applauded enthusiastically. Isadora was delighted, but Augustin Daly was furious. He thought the applause disrupted his play. From that night on, Isadora had to dance in the dark. Audiences could barely see her, much less appreciate her dancing.

After two long, miserable years with the theater troupe, Isadora finally resigned. She knew her family would get by without her meager salary. By now, her brother Raymond had joined them and was working as a journalist. Elizabeth was giving dance lessons, and Augustin was an actor. They understood and supported their sister's decision. After all, she was an artist. She needed to create her own dances.

By 1898, the Duncans had moved to a small studio apartment in Carnegie Hall. They had no furniture, only five mattresses, which they stood on end during the day so Isadora would have plenty of room to dance. Always in need of money, the Duncans often rented the studio to music teachers, who gave lessons there. Since there was only one room, the Duncans had to leave while it was being used. Years later, Isadora still remembered the whole family taking long walks through Central Park in the snow, trying to keep warm until they could go home again.

Isadora spent the next few months composing dances. Her faithful mother played the piano for hours while Isadora moved to the music. About this time, she met

A small studio in Carnegie Hall was the Duncans' home for a short time.

a young composer and pianist named Ethelbert Nevin. She was especially fond of his music and was pleased when he suggested that they perform together. She had danced at small gatherings in private homes, but now she could perform before a larger audience in a concert hall.

Their first concert, on March 24, 1898, was a great success. A few of the upper-class ladies who attended were impressed by Isadora's dancing and began inviting her to perform at their teas and garden parties. Before long, she was dancing in the drawing rooms of some of New York's wealthiest citizens. Isadora was the happiest she had been in a long time. She had the artistic freedom to create her own form of dance—and was getting paid for it.

Like the young Isadora, her dances were innocent and happy, reflecting her enthusiasm for all forms of art. She gave her dances names like *The Spirit of Spring* and *A Dance of Wandering.* To the music of Mendelssohn and Johann Baptist Strauss, she ran about the room, scattering invisible seeds or plucking imaginary flower petals. In one dance, she was a child lost in the woods; in another, she was Narcissus, blowing kisses at his reflection in a pool. Sometimes she interpreted poetry, such as Omar Khayyám's *Rubaiyat,* as her sister, Elizabeth, recited it.

The proper, tight-lipped matrons of New York society had never seen dances quite like Isadora's. But it wasn't her dancing that sent waves of shock through her audiences. It was her costume—or more accurately, her lack of costume. The slim, young Isadora ran about the stage in a shockingly filmy tunic that stopped above her knees. Her arms and legs were bare. In the eyes of these ladies, she was practically nude. They went swimming in more clothes than Isadora danced in! On at least one occasion, indignant women marched out in the middle of a performance. But either Isadora didn't notice or she didn't care. She went right on dancing—and utterly delighting those who remained in the audience.

Whether in a New York City parlor or on the lawn of a Newport, Rhode Island, summer mansion, twenty-one-year-old Isadora was attracting attention. She was a beautiful young woman with dark, expressive eyes,

Twenty-two-year-old Isadora dancing to *Rubaiyat,* by Omar Khayyám. The poem tells of a philosopher who becomes tired of the seriousness of religion and the world's problems and turns to the physical pleasures of friendship, wine, and romance—a lifestyle Isadora would embrace as an adult.

copper-red hair, and a slim, graceful body. Her performances were dramatic, passionate, and far from ordinary. To anyone watching her dance, it was obvious that Isadora loved what she was doing.

In fact, the only activity that Isadora enjoyed half as much as expressing her art was expressing her opinion, particularly when it came to the subject of ballet. Sometimes after a performance, she gave lectures with titles like "The Philosophy of the Dance." She would explain to an intrigued, though sometimes puzzled, audience what was wrong with other dancers and why her method of dance was a true art form. Dance should be natural— no turned-out feet, no tense, straight legs. Her dance was an expression of both mind and spirit, she told them, not like ballet, which separates the body from the mind.

Isadora was happy to be out of her fairy wings and creating her own dances. But she was still not completely satisfied. Dancing on the lawns of society ladies was not her idea of success. "They thought [my dancing] very charming," she said, "[but] they hadn't any of them the slightest understanding of what I was doing."

Isadora grew restless. "Just as the life in California did not satisfy me in any way," she wrote in her memoirs, "so I began to feel a strong wish to find some more congenial atmosphere than New York. And I dreamed of London, and the writers and painters one might meet there."

Once again, Isadora called the "Clan Duncan" together and convinced them it was time to move on. Fame and fortune still awaited her, but not in New York. With the exception of Augustin, who was now married, they all agreed to go with Isadora to London. There was only one problem: they had no money.

One thing the Duncan children had learned from the struggles of their childhood was how to be resourceful. Isadora wasted no time in calling on the wealthy women in whose homes she had danced. Bold and confident, she simply explained that she needed money to carry on her art in London. Her patrons must not have been as convinced of Isadora's inevitable fame as her family was. Several days and many mansions later, Isadora had only three hundred dollars—not nearly enough to get the four Duncans to London.

Finally Raymond came up with an idea. He persuaded the captain of a cattle boat to let the family sail with him to England for free. The Duncans were delighted. What an adventure! With "irrepressible merriment," they loaded their few belongings onto the boat and settled in beside the cattle pens. Not even the tiny cabin, the hard berths, or a diet of salt beef and foul-tasting tea could dampen their spirits. "Altogether it was a very happy time, in spite of the hardships," Isadora wrote, "and only the bellowings and moanings of the poor cattle in the hold depressed us." (Isadora believed it was their experience on the cattle boat that convinced Raymond to become a vegetarian, which he remained the rest of his life.)

Although the adventurous Duncans were happy to have this gift of free transportation, they were somewhat embarrassed to be making their first trip to Europe in the company of cattle. So instead of using their own names, they used Dora's mother's name: O'Gorman. Isadora called herself Maggie.

And so it was, in the spring of 1899, that Maggie O'Gorman left New York with a little money and a lot of confidence, and two weeks later, Isadora Duncan arrived in London.

III

Tuning Her Instrument

The summer of 1899 passed quickly. The four Duncans roamed the streets of London as wide-eyed as children at a circus. Each day brought a new adventure: a museum, a gallery, a concert in the park. But while they were busy enjoying the sights of London, their small supply of money was dwindling. By September, they realized they were nearly penniless.

Isadora had managed to get a few dancing jobs, but she could not earn enough to support the whole family. Finding a job as a dancer was no easy task, especially for a dancer like Isadora. She might have had better luck dancing with a ballet company or theater troupe. But Isadora wanted nothing to do with either one. Her dancing was different. She needed an audience that understood her work, and she was determined to find that audience.

In the meantime, however, something had to be done

to keep the Duncans from starving. Elizabeth had received an offer from the parents of a former student to return to New York to teach. Here was a chance to earn some money. "If I make money, I can send some to you," she told Isadora, "and as you will soon be rich and famous, I can soon rejoin you."

Without money (and Elizabeth), London quickly began to lose its charm. The weather turned cold and foggy. Instead of sightseeing, Isadora often spent the long days wrapped in blankets, sipping soup and playing checkers with her brother.

In October, Isadora's spirits were lifted somewhat by the warm days of an Indian summer. One starlit night, she and Raymond celebrated the lovely weather by dancing in the park. Unknown to them, a woman was watching them. She was both amused and impressed by the unusual sight of the dancing Duncans. She introduced herself and invited them to her lovely home in Kensington Square. By the end of the evening, Isadora had kicked off her shoes and was dancing around the parlor while her hostess played the piano.

"That meeting . . . rescued us from the state of gloom and depression into which we had fallen," Isadora wrote. That meeting was also a stroke of good luck. Their new friend turned out to be Mrs. Patrick Campbell, a well-known British actress. Mrs. Campbell introduced Isadora to London society, and before long, Isadora was again dancing in the drawing rooms of the wealthy.

Some of London's elite thought that this young woman, who danced in sandals or bare feet with filmy veils

Isadora's friendship with Mrs. Patrick Campbell, a British actress, was her ticket into the homes of London's wealthy.

swirling around her head, had created a wonderful new art form. Others found her merely an amusing novelty. Still others were shocked and dismayed. In any case, Isadora's reputation grew.

When drawing rooms and elegant parlors were no longer large enough for her growing audiences, Isadora performed in studios and intimate concert halls. Newspapers and magazines began to publish reviews of her performances. One reviewer at that time wrote: "She dances Mendelssohn's musical poem 'A Welcome to Spring' with a . . . grace that makes one think of flowers and birds and lambs at play. Her costume for this is appropriately copied from [Sandro] Botticelli's [painting] *Primavera*. . . . She is beautiful on the stage and has particularly graceful arms and hands."

Up until now, dancers used only music composed specifically for dancing, like the ballets of Pyotr Ilich Tchaikovsky. Since Isadora did not perform these traditional dances, she did not use dance music when she performed. Instead she used lyrical music—music with words—to accompany her interpretation of a poem or painting. In London, a notable music critic, J. Fuller-Maitland, saw Isadora dance and suggested that she consider eliminating the poetry readings from her programs. Instead, he told her, she should use more music—serious music, like that of Frédéric Chopin.

Isadora was intrigued by this idea. She had loved Chopin's music since her childhood days in San Francisco, but she had never considered dancing to it. No dancer had ever attempted to interpret the music of Chopin and the other great composers like Beethoven or Johann Sebastian Bach. Most people believed that such music was intended for listening, not for dancing. But unwritten rules and conventions didn't mean a thing to Isadora. She decided to follow the critic's advice.

This decision led to an important development in Isadora's dance technique. When she danced to Chopin, the music became an important part of the dance. She moved her feet, her arms, her upper body, to the rhythm of the music. Besides listening to the music with her ears, she listened with her heart, dancing to express the emotions of the music. From the seed of an idea, a new dance style began to grow.

Isadora was happy in London, but she was not one to put down roots. The slightest opportunity for a change of scenery could send her packing. When Raymond went to Paris in the summer of 1900 and begged her to follow, she didn't have to think about it for long. "He bombarded us with telegrams imploring us to come to Paris," Isadora recalled, "so one day Mother and I packed up our belongings and took the [English] Channel boat."

From the moment twenty-three-year-old Isadora stepped off the boat, she loved Paris. This was her kind of city: alive and creative. There was so much to see and do that she and Raymond would jump out of bed at five o'clock every morning to get an early start. They walked for miles all over the city and spent hours at the magnificent art museums.

Their favorite was the Louvre. Isadora was especially drawn to the Greek art collection there. Studying the vases and sculptures gave her new ideas for dances. Late at night, in front of the mirror, she practiced imitating the poses or dancing the scenes the vases illustrated. This study of Greek art made a lasting impression on Isadora and inspired much of her work in the years to come.

The art education Isadora received in Paris greatly influenced her choreography and her costumes.

Isadora posed in a
Greek tunic for this
photograph in 1903.

Isadora had come to Paris with letters of introduction
from her friends in London. Almost immediately she
began to receive invitations to dance for the fashionable
and cultured of Paris society. At that time, many Parisians enjoyed the arts and appreciated new and original
ideas. They were the *avant-garde,* and they loved this
unique young dancer from America.

Audiences were used to large groups of dancers with
magnificent scenery, but here was one woman, dancing
alone on a bare stage. Isadora wanted no scenery except
long, blue curtains. She used no props, but her audience
could almost see the invisible pool of water she dipped
her hand into or hear the imaginary violin she played.

Unlike ballet, which emphasized high, airy leaps, Isadora's dances often focused on the natural pull of gravity, using movements like kneeling or lying on the floor. Through her facial expressions and these simple movements, she portrayed joy, despair, and fear.

Isadora's circle of friends grew daily. She was free spirited and fun loving, and Paris suited her well. Isadora loved parties and fine restaurants. She also loved being flattered and admired. In France she had it all. She was painted by artists, written about by critics, wined and dined by the wealthy, and courted by admiring young men.

Paris provided Isadora with endless sources of inspiration for her work. She read Greek myths and books about dance, listened to many kinds of music, and studied great works of art. She spent long days and nights in her studio, developing her dance technique and experimenting with the music of Chopin. Often Isadora did not stop until the first hint of daylight peeked through the folds of her blue curtains.

During these first months in Paris, Isadora began to refine her theories about dance. Her dances had always been spontaneous. Now she studied each movement. She thought about how a step or a leap or a run could be used to express emotions. "The body itself must . . . be forgotten," she said. "It is only an instrument [for expressing] . . . the sentiments and thoughts of the soul."

As she worked, Isadora began to question a theory of movement that was central to ballet. This theory proposed that the base of the spine was the center for all movement. Isadora disagreed. "For hours I would stand quite still," she said, "my two hands folded between my breasts, covering the solar plexus. My mother often became alarmed to see me remain for such long intervals quite motionless as if in a trance—but I was seeking and finally discovered the central spring of all movement." This center of movement, she believed, was the solar plexus, or center of the chest. Isadora began to apply this theory to her dancing, moving forward with the upper part of the body first as no one had done before.

Newspapers continued to carry stories about Isadora's dance and the theories behind it. Some praised her, and others criticized her. But the controversy only increased her celebrity. Paris was talking about Isadora Duncan. Whether or not her theories were accepted or her dance understood, Parisians recognized her talent.

Late in 1901, when Isadora was twenty-four, the famous dancer Loie Fuller came to Isadora's studio. "Naturally I danced for her," Isadora wrote, "and explained to her all my theories, as I did for everyone and, indeed, would have done for the plumber had he come in."

Loie Fuller thought Isadora's dancing was both unique and beautiful, and she would later write in her autobiography, "[Isadora] danced with much grace—her body barely veiled by the sheerest of Greek costumes, and in particular, with bare feet. She gave promise of being someone—a promise kept." Loie invited Isadora to go with her to Germany to dance. As usual, Isadora was eager for a new experience. Paris had been good to her, but who knows, Germany might be even better.

Isadora was admired by the art community in Paris. Many famous artists made paintings and sculptures of her, including Auguste Rodin, who painted this watercolor.

The next few months were busy and exciting. Isadora danced in salons, studios, and small concert halls all over Germany and Austria. One night, after a performance in Vienna, Austria, a man came to see her. Handing her his calling card, he said, "When you wish to find a future, seek me in Budapest." His name was Alexander Grosz, a Hungarian theater manager. He offered Isadora a contract to dance for thirty evenings in a large theater in Budapest, Hungary.

Isadora had come to Europe seeking fame and fortune. Although she was getting closer to fame, she was far from fortune. Alexander's offer promised to change that. But Isadora was reluctant to dance before the public in a large theater. "My dancing is for the elite," she told him, "for the artists, sculptors, painters, musicians, but not for the general public." Alexander assured her that the public would love her. Isadora accepted his offer.

When Isadora and her mother boarded the train for Budapest one April morning in 1902, they had no idea what to expect. London and Paris had been alive with culture. Art, music, theater—the choices had been endless. What would Budapest be like?

Isadora was not disappointed. Budapest was beautiful. She enjoyed its museums and restaurants, but she was just as content to sit by her window admiring the blooming lilacs, the rolling hills, and the sparkling blue water of the Danube River. Since her childhood days spent dancing by the ocean, Isadora had used nature as a source of inspiration for her art. Budapest was rich in natural beauty, and Isadora was glad to be dancing there.

Isadora's worries about the public's reaction to her dancing were quickly put to rest. She was an instant success. At the end of her second performance, on April 20, 1902, Isadora decided to improvise a dance to Strauss's "Blue Danube Waltz." Because the Danube River ran through the city, Isadora knew the musical piece was special to the people of Budapest. But she was surprised at the overwhelming response to this impromptu dance, which was to become one of her most popular works. "The effect," she wrote, "was an electric shock. The whole audience sprang to their feet in such a delirium of enthusiasm that I had to repeat the waltz many times before they would behave less like mad people." All thirty nights, she danced in a sold-out, standing-room-only theater. Alexander Grosz had been right. Isadora Duncan had found a future.

IV

Dreams Fulfilled

Isadora would always have fond memories of Budapest, not only because her performances had been so successful there, but also because she had fallen in love with a handsome Hungarian actor. In her memoirs, she called him "Romeo," but his real name was Oscar Beregi. Being in love suited Isadora's nature perfectly. "Ah, youth and spring and Budapest and Romeo!" she wrote.

But while Isadora was content just to be in love, Oscar wanted more. He took her to look at apartments where they could live after they were married. They would settle down in Budapest, he told her, and she could quit dancing and come to watch him perform in the theater each night.

Quit dancing? This plan did not suit Isadora's nature at all. Faced with the choice between love and her art, she said good-bye to Oscar Beregi.

With the cheers and applause of the audiences of

Isadora's first love, Oscar Beregi (shown here in 1927), became a famous actor in Hungary before moving to the United States.

Budapest still ringing in her ears, Isadora set off with her new manager, Alexander Grosz, to dance in Vienna and the cities of Germany. Reactions to her dancing were mixed. While many admired her work and praised her form of dance, others continued to criticize everything from her skimpy costumes to her choice of music. On December 26, 1902, the *St. Louis Sunday Gazette* published an article about Isadora's German tour with the headline, "Isadora Duncan's Poetic Dances Have Divided Germany."

But whether praised or criticized, Isadora loved the attention—both onstage and off. Artists, poets, and students flocked to see her. Sometimes after a performance, her young admirers would unharness the horses from her carriage and pull it through the streets to her hotel. Isadora was delighted when they serenaded her outside her window until she threw them flowers or a handkerchief.

With her mother and Elizabeth to keep her company, Isadora spent the year 1903 touring Europe. Wherever she performed, not a seat in the theater remained empty. Many came simply out of curiosity; they were eager to see this scandalous young woman for themselves. But most came to enjoy her dancing. She interpreted paintings in her dances *Angel with the Violin* and *Primavera.* She expressed the emotions evoked by the music of Chopin and Christoph Gluck. And she portrayed the tragedy of death in *Death and the Maiden,* a composition performed in silence, without music. Her performances could make audiences smile with joy or weep with grief. Isadora was proving that dance could be more than mere entertainment.

Isadora dancing *Primavera* ("spring" in Italian)

As Isadora's reputation grew, so did her income. But she had never been practical, and she saw no reason to start now. She loved having money, but she loved spending it even more. She had learned to appreciate luxurious hotels, fine wines, and elegant meals. She had come a long way from the cheap boardinghouses and tomato dinners of her earlier years. As long as she had money, she was going to enjoy it to the fullest.

In the summer of 1903, just when the twenty-six-year-old dancer's career was beginning to blossom, she did something very unexpected. She canceled her tours, left her manager, and packed her bags for Greece. Shocked and disappointed, Alexander Grosz begged her to reconsider. But Isadora wouldn't listen. This trip would be the fulfillment of a dream her family had shared for many years: to relive the glory of ancient Greece, the source of all art and beauty.

Retracing the route of Ulysses in Homer's poem *Odyssey,* the Duncans set out for Athens, traveling at times by carriage, fishing boat, and on foot. "We were now all together, my mother and her four children. We decided that the Clan Duncan was quite sufficient unto itself, that other people had only led us astray from our ideals. . . . Therefore we decided that [we] should remain in Athens eternally, and there build a temple that should be characteristic of us."

Among the ruins of the Acropolis, the Duncans dressed in classical Greek tunics and danced and sang in the moonlight, sometimes embracing each other and crying tears of joy. The Greeks watched this strange American

When the Duncans found the perfect site for their temple home—a hill called Kopanos—they began to build immediately. In their haste, they didn't realize there was no water to be found. Many months of unsuccessful digging drained the Duncans' funds, and they were forced to abandon the project.

family with amusement. "They probably thought we were either drunk or crazy," Isadora wrote. But the Duncans had never cared what others thought of them. They loved Athens. This would be their home forever. But as usual, they had not decided how they would survive with no income. Forever turned out to last only one year.

When Isadora's dream of spending the rest of her life in Greece "burst like a glorious bubble," she took a train to Vienna. After a few performances there and in Munich, Germany, she settled in Berlin with her mother and sister, her white tunic, and her blue curtains.

Greece had inspired Isadora in many ways, including her choice of clothing. Both onstage and off, she now preferred to wear loose-fitting Greek tunics, robes, and sandals. Even at elegant dinner parties, where the other ladies wore formal gowns, tight-fitting corsets, and high-heeled shoes, Isadora wasn't the slightest bit embarrassed about her unusual clothing.

Isadora dancing among the ruins in Athens, Greece, in 1904

Now that Isadora was once again dancing for sold-out audiences, her manager had visions of world travel and large bank accounts. But Isadora had other ideas. "I had no wish for the triumphal world tours of which he always talked to me," she recalled. "I wanted to study, continue my researches, create a dance and movements which then did not exist, and the dream of my school, which had haunted all my childhood, became stronger and stronger."

Once Isadora made up her mind to do something, it was as good as done. If she wanted a school, she would have a school. In December 1904, with her mother and sister, she set out to find a place to house it. Less than a week later, they bought a beautiful villa in Grünewald, a suburb of Berlin.

Then Isadora went on a shopping spree. She furnished the spacious bedrooms with "forty little beds, each covered with white muslin curtains, drawn back with blue ribbons." On the wall over each bed, she hung little blue and white angels playing musical instruments. Throughout the magnificent rooms were sculptures and paintings of dancing children. The walls were painted with lilies and decorated with laurel wreaths. Isadora called it "a real children's paradise."

Isadora knew exactly how she wanted to run her school. Her pupils would live with her at the villa. When she was not touring, she would teach the dance lessons. (Elizabeth would teach in her absence.) Two governesses would help care for the children, and Elizabeth would manage the day-to-day business of running the school.

The children would be fed, clothed, educated, and given dance training without paying a penny of tuition. Isadora was interested in art, not money. She planned to help her pupils understand and appreciate her art. But she had no intention of teaching them to dance exactly like her. "The dances of no two people should be alike," she said.

Once the school was furnished and decorated to her satisfaction, Isadora prepared advertisements for the local newspapers stating that the Isadora Duncan School was now accepting "talented children." She also sent press releases to the cities where she was scheduled to perform, so that she could hold auditions when she arrived.

The response to these announcements was overwhelming. Years later, Isadora recalled how one day, returning from a matinee at a nearby theater, her carriage rounded the corner then came to a stop, unable to go any farther. The street in front of the school was filled with hopeful parents and their anxious daughters. Isadora would have no trouble filling those forty little beds.

V

Ted and Topsy

At about the same time Isadora was making plans for her new school, just before Christmas in 1904, she met someone who would change her life. That someone was Edward Gordon Craig, a well-known English stage designer. Tall and willowy, with a headful of boyish curls, he looked much younger than his thirty-two years. Like Isadora, he was an artist introducing new ideas to the world. At a time when most theater productions used elaborate stage settings, Gordon's designs were unique. Instead of intricately painted backdrops and realistic stage props, he used simple curtains and screens, indirect lighting, and few props.

Almost immediately, the two artists were attracted to one another. She called him Ted; he called her Topsy. Ted and Topsy were kindred spirits—intelligent, charming, and creative. Gordon was a man with a passion for art. He also had a passion for women. At the time he

Most people knew Edward Craig by his middle name, Gordon. Isadora called him Ted.

and Isadora first met, he was divorcing his wife, who was expecting their fourth child. He had four more children by other women.

But while some people may have seen Gordon as a scoundrel, Isadora saw him as a man with a carefree, rebellious spirit to match her own. While preparing for a brief trip to Saint Petersburg, Russia, she saw Gordon every day. By the time she boarded the train, she was writing him romantic letters.

This was Isadora's first visit to Saint Petersburg, the center of Russian ballet. The Russian people were passionate about ballet, flocking to see extravagant productions like *Swan Lake* and *The Nutcracker,* which featured large dance companies and such celebrated ballet stars as Anna Pavlova. How would they receive Isadora, who

Michel Fokine, one of many Russian ballet dancers that would be influenced by Isadora's unique style

called herself "an enemy to the ballet"? She knew it would be strange for her Russian audience "to watch a young girl, clothed in a tunic of cobweb, appear and dance before a simple blue curtain to the music of Chopin."

The Russians may have found Isadora's style strange, but they loved her performance. One reviewer wrote, "By the end of the program, the barefoot dancer had many admirers who gathered at the footlights in the dimmed hall, endlessly demanding encores."

One of her Russian admirers was Michel Fokine, a famous ballet dancer and choreographer. His later ballets showed the inspiration of Isadora's unique style by using the soft, flowing arms and loose fingers so characteristic of her dance. His choice of looser costumes and the music of Chopin also showed her influence. Other Russian choreographers would follow Fokine's lead.

Isadora was pleased that Russia liked her, but she was looking forward to returning to Berlin to see Gordon. On her way home on New Year's Eve, 1904, she wrote to him, "Darling—This darned old train is 3 hours 3 centuries 3 eternities late late late."

Back in Berlin at last, Isadora settled down to the happy task of running her school. She had chosen about twenty young girls, ages four to ten, from cities throughout Germany. (Six of these girls—Anna Denzler, Theresa Kruger, Irma Erich-Grimme, Lisa Milker, Margot Jehle, and Erika Lohmann—would stay with Isadora for many years and become her most famous pupils. They would

Isadora and her students on the steps of the Grünewald school

later be known as the Isadorables.) A warm and affectionate person, Isadora was happy to be surrounded by so many little girls, and they adored their motherly teacher. The enormous ballrooms echoed with the sounds of music and children's laughter. On sunny days, girls in tunics and sandals swayed like trees or fluttered like butterflies on the lawn.

It didn't take long for Isadora to discover that her talent was dancing, not business. She was surprised and disappointed when she realized the enormous expenses of running her school. Besides the upkeep of the villa and its beautiful gardens and the care and feeding of the girls, Isadora had to pay a large staff, including cooks, maids, a gardener, and a nurse.

Although Isadora performed regularly in Germany, her income was simply not enough to keep up with the rising expenses of the school. Something more had to be done. Elizabeth decided to form "a committee of very prominent and aristocratic women of Berlin." This committee was appropriately called the Association for the Support and Maintenance of the Dance School of Isadora Duncan.

Now Isadora was busier than ever, but she continued to see Gordon as much as possible. Although his failed relationships and illegitimate children had tarnished his reputation, Isadora saw no reason to keep her love for him a secret. When the ladies of Elizabeth's committee heard about the love affair, they were shocked.

Some of the ladies had been offended by the bare arms and legs of the little dancers at the school, but Isadora's seeming lack of morals was the last straw. Most of the committee members resigned, taking their checkbooks with them. They sent Isadora a long letter explaining that they "could no longer be patronesses of a school where the leader had such loose ideas of morals."

Isadora was furious. Who were they to judge her? She wanted a chance to respond to the committee's accusations, so she rented the entire Berlin Philharmonic Hall, supposedly to give a lecture on the dance as an expression of freedom.

Then, before a filled auditorium, she suddenly changed the subject of her speech from her freedom to dance the way she wanted to the freedom to live the way she wanted. Isadora believed that "any intelligent woman who reads the marriage contract, and then goes into it, deserves all the consequences." She had never had trouble voicing her opinions. Now she made her opinion of marriage and motherhood quite clear: Marriage deprives women of their rights, she told her startled audience. A woman should be free to "love and bear children as she [pleases]," without being forced into marriage.

"This lecture caused considerable scandal," Isadora wrote in her memoirs. "Half of the audience sympathised with me, and the other half hissed and threw anything that came to their hands on to the stage."

Isadora's speech may have made her feel better, but it did nothing to improve the financial troubles of her school. With expenses mounting, she had no choice but to tour as much as possible. She and Gordon were often separated for months at a time. Once again, the twenty-

Isadora was so amazed by her daughter, Deirdre, that she didn't mind the effects pregnancy had had on her body and her dancing. "What did I care for Art!" she wrote. "I felt I was a God, superior to any artist."

eight-year-old dancer found herself torn between career and love. "Impossible combination!" she wrote. "There began the waging of the fiercest battle that was ever known, between the genius of Gordon Craig and the inspirations of my Art."

A year after Isadora and Gordon's first meeting, in December of 1905, Isadora discovered she was pregnant. She was thrilled. Gordon was probably not so thrilled. After all, this would be his ninth child. Isadora described him as "restless, impatient, unhappy." Neither one even considered the possibility of marriage. All her life, Isadora had ignored what others thought of her. She wasn't about to start caring now. Not even the disapproval of her mother could persuade her.

Leaving Elizabeth in charge of her school, Isadora retreated to a seaside village in Holland. Gordon visited from time to time. On September 24, 1906, in a little white villa by the sea, twenty-nine-year-old Isadora gave birth to a baby girl, Deirdre. Gordon had come to be with her for the birth but left shortly afterward. Two months later, the proud mother returned to the Isadora Duncan School to show off her "youngest pupil."

VI

A Millionaire
to the Rescue

Isadora had barely unpacked her suitcase when she was faced with a familiar problem. Since she had not performed in almost a year, the Isadora Duncan School was in serious financial trouble. What could she do to save it? Isadora decided she had no choice but to tour again.

In the winter of 1907, Isadora left five-month-old Deirdre with a nurse, kissed Gordon good-bye, and set off on an exhausting tour throughout Germany, Holland, and Sweden. She missed Gordon and her baby terribly. "As you can imagine," she wrote, "it was a very sad journey for me."

But each night, when the orchestra played its first note and Isadora placed a bare foot on the carpeted stage, she would forget her sadness. With her blue curtains behind her, she played an imaginary flute, pretended to throw a spear, or climbed invisible steps to an ancient Greek temple. Her audiences were spellbound.

Although Isadora had a regular program of dances, no two performances were ever quite the same. She did not believe in memorized steps. Because she wanted to express the emotions behind her actions, she felt her dancing needed to be spontaneous. Those who saw her dance commented that it was not *what* Isadora danced that made her special, it was *how* she danced. She often told her pupils, "Don't be merely graceful. Nobody is interested in a lot of graceful young girls. Unless your dancing springs from an inner emotion and expresses an idea, it will be meaningless." Isadora practiced what she preached.

The year 1907 was difficult for Isadora. She continued to travel, returning to baby Deirdre and seeing Gordon as much as possible. But that summer she became ill and was forced to cancel many performances, putting further strain on her finances. Besides the enormous expenses of her school, Isadora helped support her mother, her sister, and sometimes her brothers. Gordon was becoming more and more dependent on her as well. His letters to her were filled with words of love and pleas for money. In August 1907, she wrote to him, "I hate to send disappointing letters and I can't send any other. . . . My money is at an end."

Gordon was moody and quick-tempered. Isadora's frequent absences made it difficult for them to try to smooth their increasingly rocky romance. To add to the problem, Gordon continued to enjoy the company of other women. Isadora was "tortured by jealousy."

By the fall of 1907, Ted and Topsy were through. "I

adored Craig," she wrote in her memoirs, "but I realized that our separation was inevitable."

To take her mind off her broken heart, Isadora put all her energy into trying to support her school. But the money she earned on her tours was simply not enough to pay the bills. Isadora didn't like the audience sitting too close to the stage, so she sometimes had the first few rows of seats removed. She also insisted on low ticket prices so that everyone could afford the pleasure of enjoying her art. Fewer seats at lower prices meant less money for Isadora. The extravagant touches she sometimes required, like hundreds of fresh lilies for an Easter program, took even more from the profits.

Isadora wanted to earn money for her school, but she

Luxuries like this Spanish shawl were hard for Isadora to live without.

was not willing to make compromises in her performances. Her frustrated manager tried to tell her how to make a profit, but Isadora insisted on doing things her way.

Determined to find the money she needed, Isadora came up with a plan: Although she had always danced solo, she would perform with some of her best pupils to show her audiences the beautiful art taught at her school. Then she would appeal to the Russian government for help. If that didn't work, she would go to another country and try again. Surely somewhere she would find the financial support she needed. So she and a small group of her young dancers, including the six Isadorables, packed their tunics and boarded a train for Russia.

First in Moscow, then in London, audiences gave them standing ovations. Critics gave them rave reviews. But no one was willing to give them money. By the summer of 1908, Isadora was becoming discouraged. "As always," she recalled, "the expenses of my little flock were enormous. Once more my bank account was nil."

Finally, she had no choice but to close her school in Grünewald. But she wasn't willing to give up completely. Somehow she would find a way to reopen it elsewhere. Reluctantly she signed a contract for a tour in the United States—without her pupils. Maybe in America she would find the support she needed for the Isadora Duncan School.

Leaving baby Deirdre with Elizabeth in Paris and her pupils at the home of a friend nearby, Isadora boarded a ship bound for New York. Just eight years had passed since she had left there on a cattle boat. "I was already famous in Europe," she wrote. "I had created an Art, a School, a Baby. Not so bad. But, as far as finances went I was not much richer than before."

Isadora's friends in Europe had warned her that Americans might not understand her art, so she was anxious to impress them. When audiences filled the Metropolitan Opera House to see her dance Beethoven's Seventh Symphony, she knew she had succeeded. In city after city, she received glowing reviews. But despite her success in the United States, she had not received the financial support she had hoped for. What would become of her pupils now? she wondered. Would she ever be able to open another school? On December 30, 1908, Isadora sailed for France. As the New York skyline faded from view, an uncertain future lay ahead of her.

Isadora was met in France by her darling Deirdre, sister Elizabeth, and the Isadorables, and she instantly forgot her troubles. "It was a splendid reunion," she later recalled, "and we danced and sang together the whole afternoon."

When the joy of her homecoming began to fade, Isadora was faced with the same old worries. One day she said jokingly to Elizabeth, "This can't go on! My banking account is overdrawn. If the School is to continue, we must find a millionaire."

In her memoirs, Isadora described what happened next: "Once I had voiced this wish, it obsessed me. 'I must find a millionaire!' I repeated a hundred times a day, first in a joke and then . . . in earnest."

One afternoon early in 1909, Isadora's search ended. Sitting in her dressing room preparing for a matinee performance, Isadora was visited by Paris Singer, heir to the Singer Sewing Machine fortune. "My maid came to me

Isadora and her millionaire, Paris Singer

with a visiting card on which I read a well-known name, and suddenly there sang in my brain: 'Here is my millionaire! Let him enter!'

"He entered, tall and blond, curling hair and beard. . . . He spoke in a charming voice, but he seemed shy. . . . 'You do not know me, but I have often applauded your wonderful art,' he said."

Isadora's handsome visitor could not have said anything more flattering than that. She was charmed by this elegant man with aristocratic manners. The father of five children and about to be divorced from his wife, Paris lived a life of luxury and extravagance. But he was as generous as he was rich. He offered to send Isadora and her pupils to the French Riviera.

Within a week, Isadora was sitting on the terrace of Paris's lovely villa, watching her pupils dance under the trees in their light blue tunics. Isadora's new patron stayed in a hotel in nearby Nice but came often to visit the children and dine with her. Under Paris's care, Isadora lived like royalty. She cruised on the Mediterranean Sea in his yacht, ate in the finest restaurants, and went to elegant parties.

That summer, thirty-two-year-old Isadora found herself in love again. She liked being indulged, and Paris indulged her like no one ever had. But although he loved her too, he neither understood nor appreciated her work. He found it difficult to understand why she took her dancing so seriously. He was often annoyed when she spent time away from him to rehearse or perform. This was a conflict all too familiar to Isadora.

Then, in September 1909, Isadora discovered that she was expecting another baby. She had a strong feeling that her new baby was a boy.

Although Paris already had a large family, he was delighted at the prospect of having a child with Isadora, and he indulged and pampered her more than ever. Some time earlier, Isadora had signed a contract for a second tour in the United States. She saw no reason to stop performing just because she was pregnant. Elizabeth was setting up a dance school of her own in Darmstadt, Germany, and agreed to let Isadora's pupils stay with her there. In October, Isadora left Deirdre and her pupils with her sister and set sail with Paris for America.

"The tour in America was most happy, successful, and prosperous," Isadora recalled. Again she was well received by American audiences. But soon her pregnancy became too obvious under her scanty costumes— even for the most open-minded in the audience—and Isadora decided it was best to end her tour. She gave her last performance at Carnegie Hall in New York City on December 2, 1909. Six days later, the excited couple sailed for France to await the birth of their child.

VII

Tragedy

Just as she had predicted, Isadora gave birth to a son. Patrick Duncan was born on the first day of May, 1910, in a rented mansion on the French Riviera. Paris was delighted with his new son and was eager to marry his beloved Isadora. But Isadora had not changed her opinion of marriage. "How stupid for an artist to be married," she told him, "and as I must spend my life making tours round the world, how could you spend your life in the stage-box admiring me?"

"You would not have to make tours if we were married," he answered. She would never have to worry about money again. Clearly, this man did not understand Isadora. No, she said, she loved him but she would not marry him. Their relationship was fine just the way it was.

Early in 1911, Isadora returned to the United States to fulfill a third contract. Her trip was brief but successful.

Patrick Duncan,
1910

She performed two new dances, which she called *The Dances of the Furies.* In Greek mythology, the Furies were the spirits of revenge who pursued those who had committed crimes.

In these compositions, Isadora used ugliness and weightiness for expression. Her elbows jutted out sharply. Her fingers were hooked like claws. Her mouth gaped in a silent scream. She emphasized gravity by dropping heavily to the floor and staggering under the weight of an invisible boulder.

Dancing that used ugliness for expression had never been seen before. The twisted movements and heaviness of these dramatic dances would inspire many modern dancers in the years to come. *The Dances of the Furies* would be two of Isadora's most influential works.

When she had fulfilled her obligations in the United States, Isadora returned to France and settled into a house with a large studio in Neuilly, outside of Paris. The next two years were probably the most settled years of her life. She traveled as little as possible, preferring to perform close to home. "I was quite happy," she wrote, "and dreaded any more tours which would separate me from the children."

Isadora covered the walls of the studio with her blue
curtains and hired a pianist to come in each day to play
for her. On warm summer days, she danced with the
doors opened wide so she could watch her children playing happily in the garden.

Despite her peaceful home life, Isadora's relationship
with Paris was becoming more and more turbulent. She
seemed to enjoy flaunting her independence by flirting
with other men, and this angered Paris so much that he
would often leave for weeks or months at a time.

Early in 1913, Isadora had several experiences that left
her feeling uneasy and frightened. In January, on a brief
tour in Russia, she looked at piles of snow along the side
of the road and saw a vision: two rows of children's cof-
fins. On the same tour, while riding a train, she heard
music in her head all night. She wrote to a friend,
"[I] heard Chopin's 'Funeral March' all through the night
and I had a sort of vision that impressed me so much

Isadora with Deir-
dre, left, and Patrick
in 1913

that I danced it the following evening, just as I had seen it, without a rehearsal."

These experiences left Isadora disturbed and consumed with thoughts of death. Returning to France and her children eased her worries a bit, but soon her strange visions returned. This time, she began to see three black-birds flying about her studio each night. Frayed nerves and sleepless nights finally drove her to consult a doctor, who advised her to take a rest in the country. Isadora was only too happy to comply. She longed for some quiet time with Deirdre and Patrick.

The three Duncans, along with the children's governess, drove to Versailles, ten miles outside of Paris. Isadora was performing a series of concerts in the city, and Versailles was close enough that she could drive in for rehearsals and performances.

The Isadorables had been attending Elizabeth's dancing school in Germany, and Isadora had not seen them for some time, so she requested that they come to Paris to perform with her. These six young women were deeply devoted to Isadora and her dance—so devoted, in fact, that Irma, Lisa, and Anna had changed their surnames to "Duncan." They had spent most of their lives studying Isadora's dance and, by now, knew her techniques perfectly.

Their performance with Isadora in Paris was a happy reunion for dancers and audience alike. One reviewer wrote, "Six slender young girls appeared on the scene attired in rose-colored scarves and crowned with flowers. Bare-limbed and light-footed, they threw themselves

The six Isadorables, posing with Isadora (center, seated) in 1917. At this time, the young women were beginning to demand more personal and professional independence from their teacher. This made Isadora angry and jealous of their youth.

fully into the dance. . . . Isadora dances with them and is part of them."

A few weeks later, on April 19, 1913, Isadora received a telephone call from Paris Singer. He invited her to bring the children to lunch with him, and she gladly accepted. Deirdre, now six, and Patrick, almost three, were excited about the trip. The Duncans hadn't seen Patrick's father in several months.

The foursome enjoyed a lively lunch at an Italian restaurant in the city. Afterward, Isadora stayed in Paris for a rehearsal. But the children were tired, and Isadora decided they should return to Versailles to rest. She gave each of her children a kiss and helped them into a hired limousine. When little Deirdre pressed her lips against the car window, Isadora leaned forward and kissed the glass. She would later recall how the touch of the cold, hard glass against her lips left her with an uneasy feeling. Then she went into her studio to rest before her rehearsal.

A short while later, Isadora was startled by the sudden arrival of Paris in her studio. In her memoirs, she wrote, "[Paris] was there, staggering like a drunken man. His knees gave way—he fell before me—and from his lips came these words: 'The children—the children—are dead!'"

Isadora refused to believe it. She told him it could not be true. But it was true. Her horrible visions of death had become a reality. Her children were dead. On the way back to Versailles, their car had stalled, and the driver had gotten out to turn the crank in front (which is how cars were started in those days). When the motor started, the car lurched and then began to roll backward. The driver tried to grab the door, but the car gathered speed, and as he watched in horror, it plunged into the Seine River. The children and their governess drowned.

Isadora was consumed by a sorrow from which she would never fully recover. She sent a telegram to Gordon Craig, Deirdre's father:

> OUR LITTLE GIRL DEIRDRE WAS TAKEN FROM US TODAY WITHOUT SUFFERING. MY BOY PATRICK IS TAKEN WITH HER. THIS SORROW IS BEYOND ANY WORDS. I SEND MY ETERNAL UNDYING LOVE. ISADORA.

News of Isadora's tragedy spread quickly. Friends

The funeral procession for Deirdre and Patrick

came to comfort her. Letters and telegrams poured into her home from all over the world. Even those who knew her only as the famous Isadora Duncan were so touched by her grief that they stood weeping in the streets. Flowers filled every room and spilled out into the street. Students from a nearby art school covered the trees and bushes in her garden with white roses and lilacs.

Isadora's grief was almost unbearable. She turned to Paris Singer for solace, but he too was suffering. "My intense yearning—my sorrow—were too strong for [him] to stand," she wrote. "One morning he left abruptly, without warning."

Isadora's brothers and sister tried to comfort her, taking her with them to Greece and Albania. But nothing could ease her pain. All alone, she drove hundreds of miles—to Switzerland, back to France, then over the Alps to Italy. There, late in the fall of 1913, she settled down at the home of a close friend, Eleanora Duse. Isadora spent her days wandering by the sea and her nights unable to sleep, counting the minutes until daylight. For the first time in her life, she could not even think of dancing. She wrote to a friend, "I know that my real self died with my children. . . . And now I feel that my life and my art died with them."

One cold, gray afternoon, as Isadora walked by the sea, she thought she saw Deirdre and Patrick holding hands and skipping ahead of her along the beach. She ran after them, calling their names. Suddenly, the visions of her dead children disappeared, leaving Isadora staring in disbelief at the empty beach.

"I had for some moments the distinct feeling that I was with one foot over the line which divides madness from sanity," she wrote. Overcome with fear and sadness, she lay down on the cold, wet sand and wept.

Isadora had no idea how long she had been there when she was suddenly aware of a hand on her head. She looked up to see an acquaintance of Eleanora, a young Italian sculptor named Romano Romanelli. "Why are you always weeping?" he asked her. "Is there nothing I can do for you—to help you?"

Isadora believed that only another child could console her, and here was a handsome young man. "Yes," she replied. "Save me—save more than my life—my reason."

Romano invited her to visit him at his studio, and Isadora gratefully accepted. She was glad to have someone to talk to. Soon the two were strolling along the beach and talking for hours in his studio.

Almost as quickly as their relationship had begun, it ended. Isadora's young sculptor was engaged to be married to another woman. Although she hadn't known of his engagement, Isadora wasn't angry. Their brief love affair had "rescued [her] from grief and death."

Not long afterward, Isadora learned that she was expecting another baby. She was filled with a calm and comforting happiness, for she believed that this new baby was the spirit of Deirdre or Patrick coming back to her. "I felt that my children's spirits hovered near me, that they would return to console me on earth," she said.

As the cold days of winter approached, Isadora moved to Rome. There, early in 1914, she received a telegram from Paris Singer asking her to return to France. She gratefully accepted his invitation.

Isadora arrived to find an elegant hotel suite filled with flowers waiting for her. Paris must have loved her a great deal. He was happy to see her, and despite his past jealousies, he was not upset by the news of her pregnancy. Instead he offered her a gift that would bring her further relief from her sorrow. He had bought her a large hotel at Bellevue, on the outskirts of Paris, for her school.

Nothing could have revived Isadora like this generous gift. The next morning, she went right to work "transforming this rather banal hotel to a Temple of the Dance of the Future." At last, Isadora Duncan had returned to her art.

VIII

Dancing Again

Isadora's new school at Bellevue was magnificent. High on a hill overlooking Paris, with two hundred rooms (eighty of them bathrooms!), it was surrounded by gardens that sloped down to the Seine River below. Isadora kept herself busy decorating the enormous rooms and preparing for classes to begin. With the help of the six Isadorables, she was soon teaching classes to fifty children.

It had been a long time since she had known the happiness she felt when her little pupils called out together, "Good morning, Isadora." But her renewed happiness was brief. Tension was mounting between the nations of Europe, and by the end of July 1914, France was at war with Germany. The future of her school, of France, of the world, was suddenly uncertain.

In the midst of this uncertainty, on August 1, 1914, thirty-seven-year-old Isadora gave birth to a son. Alone with her tiny newborn for the first time, Isadora whispered, "Who are you, Deirdre or Patrick? You have returned to me."

Sadly, only a few hours after birth, the infant died. "I believe that in that moment I reached the height of any suffering that can come to me on earth," she wrote.

Isadora felt hopeless about her future and lacked the enthusiasm to return to her teaching. Her many happy years in France had given her a strong sense of patriotism for her beloved country, and she decided to offer her school to be used as a hospital for wounded soldiers.

Many of Isadora's pupils returned to their families. The rest, about seventeen of them, were sent away from warring Europe to stay with Augustin in New York. (Elizabeth and her school had also left Europe and were settled in Tarrytown, New York.) When Isadora was well enough to travel, she too left for the United States, arriving in New York City on November 24, 1914.

More than anything, Isadora wanted to put her sorrows behind her and dance again. But for the first time in her life, she faced a new obstacle: stage fright. Isadora had spent her life dancing in front of people. Now she was terrified. Her first public performance since the death of her children (and the American debut of the Isadorables) was scheduled for December 3, 1914, at Carnegie Hall. As the day drew nearer, Isadora wondered if she would be able to do it.

Not only did she do it, but she performed one of the most memorable dances of her career: Franz Schubert's "Ave Maria." She had composed two versions, one as a solo, with herself as the Virgin Mary, and one as a group performance, with her pupils as adoring angels. This was the most religious dance Isadora had ever composed. Perhaps it was an expression of her personal feelings at the time, for her performance that December evening was so moving the audience wept. Isadora would perform the *Ave Maria* many times in the years that followed.

Isadora had conquered her stage fright as well as the hearts of New York audiences. After one of her performances, she received twenty-seven curtain calls.

In May 1915, Isadora returned to Europe. She hoped the war would end soon so that she and her pupils could return to Bellevue, but the war raged on. Isadora borrowed money to send her pupils to a boarding school in Switzerland, while she stayed on in Paris.

The atmosphere in Paris was as sad and gloomy as Isadora's mood. To help lift her spirits, she needed the company of people. Her apartment became a gathering place for friends and fellow artists. Soldiers home on leave were welcome there and were often treated to a performance by Isadora. She turned no one away. With her usual extravagance, she provided food and drink for anyone who showed up. In the meantime, she was desperately trying to find the funds to support her pupils in Switzerland.

In the spring of 1916, moved by the sight of the lonely, wounded soldiers returning from the war front, Isadora volunteered to dance at a war-charity benefit concert. This would be her first public appearance in Paris since the death of her children, and she wanted this perfor-

Isadora performed at several war-charity benefit concerts during the war, this one in 1918 for the Italian Relief Fund.

mance to be one that the people of Paris would never forget. She composed three new dances, performed to Cesar Franck's *Rédemption,* Tchaikovsky's *Pathetique* Symphony, and "La Marseillaise" (the French national anthem).

Although all three dances would later be considered among Isadora's greatest works, it was *La Marseillaise* that brought the French to their feet that night. French forces were clashing with the German army at that very moment, struggling to keep enemy forces away from Paris. Isadora, dressed in a blood-red tunic, danced alone, yet she represented an entire nation at arms, bravely facing the enemy. One reviewer said of her performance that night, "Isadora Duncan has found the heart of Paris again."

La Marseillaise was moving for both the audience and the performer. Isadora saw this dance as a tribute to France, which she thought of as her home despite her American roots.

Passionately patriotic, *La Marseillaise* was Isadora's first political composition. From that night on, she would experiment with many dances that made political and social statements. Never before had dance been used for such purposes. Isadora Duncan was paving the way for future dancers and choreographers to express their political views through their art.

From 1918 to early 1920, Isadora performed all over the world, while the Isadorables (now renamed the Isadora Duncan Dancers) toured in the United States. In her memoirs, she wrote, "Fine art comes from the human spirit," and certainly her dancing during these years reflected this belief. After so much tragedy in her life, she no longer seemed interested in creating the gay and carefree dances of her youth. Her work now was more mature, serious, and sad. Just as the death of her children had inspired her religious dances, the war inspired her patriotic and political dances.

During this time, Isadora fell in love with her piano accompanist, Walter Rummel. Years later, she wrote, "Each love affair in my life would have made a novel, and they all ended badly." This was certainly true with Walter. After five of the six Isadora Duncan Dancers returned to Europe to dance with Isadora in June 1920 (Erika had dropped out of the group to study painting), Walter became involved with the young and beautiful Anna. By the spring of 1921, Anna had left the group, taking Walter with her. When Margot became ill and unable to dance, the six Isadora Duncan Dancers were reduced to three: Theresa, Irma, and Lisa.

For the first time in many years, Isadora was alone—no lover, no family, no school full of pupils to keep her company. Sixteen years had passed since the first Isadora Duncan School had opened in Germany. During those years, Isadora had known love, joy, and tragedy. But she had never given up hope for her school. In a letter to Irma, she wrote, "Before I die, at least one hundred beings must understand the work and give it to others."

In 1920, on a trip with her six pupils, Isadora concentrated on teaching them "Beauty, Calm, Philosophy and Harmony." Inwardly, she was devastated over the relationship between Anna and her former suitor, Walter Rummel.

Now forty-four years old, perhaps Isadora was feeling more and more the need to pass on her art to young dancers. Even though Isadora had loaned Bellevue to the war effort, France was unwilling to help her open a new school after the war. So Isadora turned to a country that appreciated the arts and had always welcomed her: Russia. She wrote to the Russian government, asking for a studio, a house, "simple food, simple tunics, and the opportunity to give our best work." She wanted to "dance for the masses, for the working people who need my art and have never had the money to come to see me."

A short time later, Isadora received a telegram. As she read the words, her heart nearly burst with joy.

COME TO MOSCOW. WE WILL GIVE YOU YOUR SCHOOL
AND A THOUSAND CHILDREN.

The Russians received a response right away. Yes, Isadora Duncan, the famous barefoot dancer, would come to Moscow.

Just before leaving, Isadora visited a fortune-teller. "You are bound on a long journey," the fortune-teller told her. "You will have many strange experiences, you will have troubles, you will marry—"

"But at the word 'marry,'" Isadora recalled, "I cut her short with laughter. I, who was always against marriage? I would never marry."

The fortune-teller simply replied, "Wait and see."

IX

The Russian
Years

On July 12, 1921, Isadora boarded the SS *Baltanic,* bound for Russia. Of the three remaining Isadora Duncan Dancers, only Irma was willing to go with Isadora on this new adventure. More than anything, Isadora wanted to believe that this time her school would become the "temple" she had spent her life trying to build.

The Russian government presented Isadora with a two-story mansion in Moscow that featured rosewood columns, gold molding, marble staircases, and a staff of sixty, including a doctor, a cook, a typist, and even a plumber. Her staff also included Ilya Schneider, a Russian man who served as Isadora's interpreter and secretary and helped manage the school. Isadora was presented with 150 children, from whom she selected 40 to attend her school.

Within a few months, Isadora and Irma were ready to begin teaching classes. Isadora didn't speak a word of

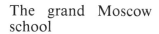

The grand Moscow school

Russian, but she needed no words to show the children how to flutter like leaves in the wind or move as gracefully as flowing water. The Russian children loved their new dance lessons and thrived under Isadora's direction.

Soon the children were ready to give their first performance. The night of November 7, 1921, was the fourth anniversary of the Russian Revolution, which had freed Russia from a controlling czar, or king, and had led to the formation of the Soviet Union. The audience at the Bolshoi Theater was bustling with excitement over the opportunity to see Isadora Duncan and her pupils perform on this special night. All three thousand seats of the theater were filled. Even the Communist leader, Vladimir Ilyich Lenin, was there for the occasion.

In honor of the revolution's anniversary, Isadora danced a solo to Tchaikovsky's "Marche Slav." In this dance, she portrayed a slave, a symbol for the Russian people. With her hands bound behind her back by invisible chains, she struggled, then stumbled and fell to her knees. But before the dance ended, she had broken her chains and freed herself.

Although Isadora had created this dance almost four years earlier, this was the first time she had performed it before a Russian audience. Their response was overwhelming. The crowd rose to their feet, cheering. Among them, Lenin shouted, "Bravo, bravo, Miss Duncan!"

The *Marche Slav* was a significant dance of social protest. Like *La Marseillaise,* it would have a profound influence on dance choreography in later years by inspiring other dancers to compose dances with political and social themes.

Her warm reception made Isadora wonder if she had found a home in the Soviet Union. But shortly after her

The *Marche Slav* began with Isadora's hands tied behind her back by invisible chains.

magnificent performance at the Bolshoi Theater, she received some devastating news: A sudden change in political policy had eliminated the aid the government had promised her. There was no more money for her school. She was welcome to stay in the Soviet Union, but she would have to support her school herself.

Isadora felt cheated and betrayed. Now she was faced with a decision. Should she abandon the school and return to Europe, or should she go on tour to raise the money to keep her Russian school alive? She had struggled too long and too hard to give up her school. She decided to tour.

The school wasn't Isadora's only reason for wanting to stay in the Soviet Union. She had fallen in love again, this time with a famous Russian poet fifteen years younger than she. Sergei Esenin was an artist, and Isadora had always understood artists. However, he spoke only Russian. Isadora still knew very little Russian, so she attended daily lessons. One day, her elderly teacher was shocked and embarrassed when Isadora told her, "You'd better teach me what I ought to say to a beautiful man when I want to kiss him."

In the spring of 1922, Isadora had a chance to make another tour in America. She needed the income, but she wanted Sergei to go with her. Unfortunately, this presented a problem.

Many Americans did not like Russians. These Americans believed that the Soviet Union's Communist government opposed the ways of the United States's democratic government. Thinking Sergei might be in danger in the

United States, the Soviet government was reluctant to allow such a popular and highly valued poet to go there.

Also, Isadora knew that Americans would consider it improper for her to travel with a man who was not her husband. When she toured the United States with Paris Singer in 1909, Americans seemed to pretend not to notice. But Paris was an American millionaire. Americans might not be so forgiving of a poor Russian like Sergei. If Americans did not approve of Isadora and Sergei, they were not likely to donate money to her school.

Isadora knew that the only answer was to marry Sergei. Having an American wife would give him legal protection in a country hostile to Russians. Isadora had opposed marriage all her life. Not even the birth of her three children had changed her mind. But now she gave in.

Conveniently, however, the Soviet marriage contract was quite fair. Neither husband nor wife was financially responsible for the other, and the marriage could be annulled, or ended, by either person, at any time and for any reason. In case anyone thought she had acted against her principles, Isadora told reporters, "Such a marriage [of equal partners] is the only convention to which any free-minded woman could consent, and is the only form of marriage to which I have ever subscribed."

On May 2, 1922, Isadora and Sergei were married. The next day, with her school in the capable hands of Irma and Ilya, Isadora and Sergei left Moscow. Seeing them off at the airport was a busload of her pupils, bearing a large sign that read: "A free spirit can exist only in a free body! Duncan School."

Irma, left, with Isadora and Sergei on their wedding day, May 2, 1922

The fortune-teller's unbelievable prediction had come true. Unfortunately, she had not predicted that Isadora's marriage would be doomed from the start. Sergei's boyish charm quickly disappeared. He was spoiled, temperamental, and jealous of his wife's fame. He also drank heavily, and in fits of anger, he hurled insults—and sometimes a lamp or table—at Isadora. Isadora realized she had made a terrible mistake.

To make matters worse, traveling in the United States was not pleasant. Although neither Isadora nor Sergei were Communists, they were treated with suspicion and even hatred. Reporters followed the dancer everywhere. When she realized they were not interested in her art, Isadora became impatient and even rude. They wanted gossip and scandal. Isadora's drunken Russian husband, her scanty costumes, and her unconventional lifestyle provided plenty of that. A well-known evangelist named Billy Sunday blasted Isadora from his pulpit. "That Bolshevik hussy doesn't wear enough clothes to pad a crutch!" he shouted.

Isadora could not understand this preoccupation with her costumes, and she delighted the hungry press by defending herself. "Why should I care what part of my body I reveal?" she said. "Why is one part more evil than another? Is not all body and soul an instrument through which the artist expresses his inner message of beauty?"

By January 1923, just three months after her arrival in the United States, Isadora had had enough. She and Sergei boarded a ship for Europe. In her usual dramatic style, she called to reporters gathered to see her off, "Goodbye, America. I shall never see you again."

Isadora hoped her relationship with Sergei would improve when they returned to Russia. It didn't. His drinking got heavier, their arguments became fiercer, and Isadora's spirits sank lower. Sergei began to disappear for days at a time. His absences became longer and more frequent, and by the fall of 1923, the couple was living apart.

On her own again, Isadora felt an almost exhilarating sense of freedom. She could now get on with her work. In a burst of creative energy, she composed a group of dances to seven revolutionary songs. These works, like the *Marche Slav,* would have a significant impact on the social protest dances popular in the United States in the 1930s and 1940s. Such dancers as Martha Graham, Doris Humphrey, and Helen Tamiris would later use political revolution as a theme for their dance compositions.

In the fall of 1924, Isadora began touring again. Irma and Ilya were doing a fine job running the Russian school, but as always, the school was struggling financially. Her earnings were not even enough to pay for fuel to heat the enormous building during the frigid Russian winter. The studios were often so cold that classes had to be canceled. Even food was becoming scarce.

But Isadora wasn't ready to give up. That winter, Isadora decided to begin writing her memoirs in hopes that she could earn some much-needed money. In a letter to Irma, she called the project "my only hope."

The following year brought more sorrow to Isadora's

life. Margot, one of the six original Isadora Duncan Dancers, died. These pupils had been like daughters to Isadora, and Margot's death must have awakened the terrible memories of the loss of Deirdre and Patrick twelve years earlier. Then, in December 1925, Sergei committed suicide. Although he and Isadora had been apart for two years, she was still very saddened by his death.

For the next year, Isadora gave a few concerts, corresponded with Irma about the Russian school, and made halfhearted plans to open a new school in France.

Now forty-nine years old, Isadora had dyed her white hair to keep it copper red, and she had grown quite heavy. But although Isadora had lost her girlish figure, she had not lost her charm. She was still surrounded by handsome men. "I love potatoes and young men, that's my trouble!" she once told a friend. As always, she was

By 1927, Isadora had lost her children, her husband, and her girlish figure. But she continued to dance and enjoy the finer things in life.

plagued by money troubles and managed to convince someone else to pay for the luxuries she enjoyed. Even Paris Singer was still lending her money.

She continued to dance, though one critic wrote of her performance at this time, "Her art was seen to have changed. . . . Across her face, tilting this way and that, flee the mortal looks of tragedy, knowledge, love, scorn, pain." Isadora had certainly known all of those and more in her life.

One day in September 1927, Isadora saw a beautiful red Bugatti sports car at a garage in Nice, France. A friend, Victor Seroff, suggested that she should pretend she was interested in buying the car so that the garage owner would let her have a ride. Isadora must have liked that idea, because on September 14, she asked for a driver to bring the Bugatti to her hotel.

Isadora was in good spirits that day. Waiting in her hotel room with some friends, she put a record on the phonograph and danced happily around the room. When the car arrived, she threw a favorite red-fringed shawl around her shoulders and ran downstairs. One friend suggested that the shawl was not warm enough, but Isadora wouldn't listen. She leaped gaily into the car and, with a smile and a wave, called out in French, "Farewell, my friends, I go to glory."

When the car started moving, Isadora's shawl became tangled in the spokes of one of the wheels and tightened around her neck. Within seconds, Isadora Duncan was dead. As if she had written her own death scene, Isadora died as dramatically as she had lived.

Isadora had devoted her life to proving that dance was a creative art like the paintings, music, sculpture, and literature that inspired her. Although she did not live to see the effects of her revolutionary style of dance, almost everything about her work, from her choice of music and costume to her spontaneous, natural movements, inspired the dancers and choreographers who followed her.

Considered by many to be the mother of modern dance, Isadora Duncan was a true original, both in her life and in her art. But for Isadora, life and art were one. "My Art is just an effort to express the truth of my being in gesture and movement," she wrote in her memoirs. "From the first, I have only danced my life."

Afterword

After Isadora's death, Irma Duncan continued to run the Russian school, assisted by Ilya Schneider. Students from this school performed Isadora's dances in cities all over the Soviet Union.

From December 1928 to January 1930, Irma and a group of dancers from the school toured the United States as a tribute to Isadora, giving four hundred performances in seventy-eight cities. Of those performances, *Dance Magazine* said, "The idea by which the valiant and uncomparable Isadora lived and breathed and worked was as present on that stage as if that genius herself stood in the wings and urged her followers on."

The tour with Irma ended abruptly when the Soviet government demanded that the dancers return to Moscow. Angered by such a demand, Irma quit her position with the school and remained in the United States. Ilya continued to run the Russian school until it closed in 1949.

No single Isadora Duncan school exists as it once did. Duncan dancers and centers of dance are scattered throughout the United States and the world. These dancers give concerts and gather at national and international

Irma Duncan, right, and the Isadora Duncan Dancers of Moscow, performing *Dubinushka* ("Workman's Song") on their American tour

festivals, where they recreate Isadora's unique dances.

But no school is needed to see the legacy Isadora Duncan left behind. Her treatment of music, her political works, her attention to classical Greece, and above all, her total freedom of body and emotion helped turn her dream of a "different dance" into a reality. In modern dance, the spirit of the barefoot dancer lives on.

Notes

page 7

Several of Isadora's biographers claim that her given name was Dora Angela, after her mother, Mary Dora. But baptismal records from St. Mary's Church in San Francisco give her name as Angela I., for Angela Isadora. The baptismal records also show Isadora's year of birth as 1877. Because Isadora's birth records were destroyed in the San Francisco earthquake and fire of 1906, Augustin Duncan appeared in California Superior Court in 1947 to verify Isadora's birth date as 1878. Raymond Duncan, however, insisted that the date on the baptismal record was correct.

page 42

Although Isadora advertised for "talented *children*," almost all of the hundreds of pupils who attended Isadora's schools were girls. Isadora's techniques were created primarily for females and were never altered to accommodate the male physique or to present a more masculine image. Ilya Schneider confirms that for a brief time, there were a few boys at the Russian school. However, Isadora's female-oriented dance technique, as well as the need for separate sleeping quarters, made it impractical to let the boys stay.

page 47

The name "Isadorables" was coined sometime between 1909 and 1911 by Fernand Divoire, a French poet and dance critic who followed Isadora's career closely. The group liked it so much they adopted it. They were renamed the "Isadora Duncan Dancers" about 1918.

page 52

Isadora continued to correspond with Gordon Craig until 1920. They also saw each other from time to time.

page 56

In her autobiography, Isadora refers to Paris Singer as "Lohengrin," or simply "L."

page 62

Anna Duncan claimed that all of the Isadorables except Erika Lohmann changed their names to Duncan. Victor Seroff, a friend of Isadora, wrote that Anna, Irma, and Theresa were the only ones to do so. However, biographer Lillian Loewenthal, who has carefully studied the lives of Isadora's pupils, reports that only Anna, Irma, and Lisa used the name Duncan.

page 71

"La Marseillaise" is pronounced LAH mahr-say-YEZ.

page 72

In 1918, Isadora decided to legally adopt her six "disciples" in order to give the young women, who were German, a legal American connection. This connection would allow them to travel freely in the United States during the war. The adoptions were finalized in 1920.

page 82

Isadora died before completing her memoirs. Several of the biographers who knew her claim that parts of *My Life* were either made up or exaggerated by Isadora in an effort to please the publishers and make her book more inviting to the public. In addition, some people, including Gordon Craig, claim that Isadora's memoirs were altered after her death. Since she died before the book was published, she never saw the final manuscript.

Bibliography

Blair, Fredrika. *Isadora.* New York: McGraw-Hill Book Co., 1986.

Dillon, Millicent. *After Egypt: Isadora Duncan and Mary Cassatt.* New York: Dutton, 1990.

Duncan, Isadora. *My Life.* New York: Liveright Publishing Corporation, 1927.

Kendall, Elizabeth. *Where She Danced.* New York: Knopf, 1979.

Kozodoz, Ruth. *Isadora Duncan: Dancer.* New York: Chelsea House Publishers, 1988.

Loewenthal, Lillian. *The Search for Isadora: The Legend and Legacy of Isadora Duncan.* Pennington, N.J.: Princeton Book Company, 1993.

MacDougall, Allan Ross. *Isadora: A Revolutionary in Art and Love.* New York: Thomas Nelson & Sons, 1960.

Schneider, Ilya Ilyich. *Isadora Duncan: The Russian Years.* New York: Harcourt, Brace and World, Inc., 1968.

Seroff, Victor. *The Real Isadora.* New York: Dial Press, 1971.

Steegmuller, Francis. *"Your Isadora": The Love Story of Isadora Duncan and Gordon Craig Told Through Letters and Diaries.* New York: Vintage Books, 1976.

Terry, Walter. *Isadora Duncan: Her Life, Her Art, Her Legacy.* New York: Dodd, Mead & Co., 1963.

All quotations in this book were taken from the above sources. Most were selected from Isadora Duncan's autobiography, *My Life.*

Index

All illustrations are reproduced through the courtesy of the New York Public Library for the
Performing Arts except: The Bettmann Archives, pp. 63, 71, 93; Bibliothèque Nationale, p. 60;
Carnegie Hall Archives, p. 19; Culver Pictures, p. 26; Library of Congress, front cover
(portrait), back cover, pp. 55, 65, 72; Museum of the City of New York, p. 77; Philadelphia
Museum of Art (given by Jules E. Mastbaum), p. 32; San Francisco Performing Arts Library
and Museum, front cover (line drawing), pp. 6, 11, 73; Special Collections, Research Libraries,
UCLA, p. 44; UPI/Bettmann, pp. 36, 45, 94.

About the Author

Barbara O'Connor grew up in South Carolina wearing tap shoes, and she took them with her to college at the University of South Carolina. After graduating with a degree in English, Ms. O'Connor moved to Los Angeles, where she lived for many years. She now lives in Duxbury, Massachusetts, with her husband, Bill, and her son, Grady. She still pulls out those tap shoes regularly for classes in nearby Boston.

Ms. O'Connor is the author of *Mammolina: A Story about Maria Montessori.* She is now delving into the life of World War II reporter Ernie Pyle, who will be the subject of her third book.